Burdett Surname

Ireland: 1600s to 1900s

From Ireland Church Records of Baptism, Marriage and Death

Comprised of Roman Catholic and Church of Ireland Records

From Counties Carlow, Cork, Kerry and Dublin City

Compiled by **Donovan Hurst**

April 8, 2013

ISBN: 1939958156
ISBN-13: 978-1-939958-15-0

Dedication

This work is dedicated to all of those that came before us and shaped our lives to make us the people that we are today.

Table of Contents

Introduction

This is a compilation of individuals who have the surname of Burdett that lived in the country of Ireland from the 1600s to the 1900s. I have placed each entry into one of four categories: Families, Individual Births/Baptisms, Individual Burials, and Individual Marriages. If a marriage entry primarily concerns an Individual Burdett whom is female, then I have placed that entry under the category of Individual Marriages. If a marriage entry primarily concerns an Individual Burdett whom is male, then I have placed that entry under the category of Families. Images of many of these listings are available at http://churchrecords.irishgenealogy.ie/churchrecords/.

To help guide the reader of this work, the format of this book is as follows:

- Main Family Entry (Husband and Wife) (Father and Mother)

  o Child of Main Family Entry, including Spouse(s) when available

    ▪ Grandchild of Main Family Entry, including Spouse(s) when available

      • Great-Grandchild of Main Family Entry, including Spouse(s) when available

(**Bolded Text**) following any entry includes any additional information such as Residence(s), Occupation(s), Signature(s), etc. when available.

Hurst

Some of the fonts used in this work symbolizes Celtic writing. The traditional letters, numbers, and punctuation marks and their Celtic counterparts are as follows:

Traditional Letters (Uppercase & Lowercase)

A a B b C c D d E f G g H h I i J j K k L l M m N n O o P p Q q R r S s T t U u V v W w X x Y y Z z

Celtic Letters (Uppercase & Lowercase)

A a B b C c D ð E e F f G g H h I i J j K k L l M m

N n O o P p Q q R r S s T t U u V v W w X x Y y Z z

Traditional Numbers

1 2 3 4 5 6 7 8 9 10

Celtic Numbers

1 2 3 4 5 6 7 8 9 10

Traditional Punctuation

. , : ' " & - ( )

Celtic Punctuation

. , : ' " & - ( )

Parish Churches

Carlow (Church of Ireland)

Carlow Parish.

Cork & Ross

(Roman Catholic or RC)

Lislee, Abbeymahon & Donoughmore (Barryroe) Parish.

Dublin (Church of Ireland)

Clontarf Parish, St. Andrew Park Parish, St. Anne Parish, St. George Parish, St. Mary Parish, St. Michan Parish, St. Nicholas Without Parish, St. Patrick Parish, St. Paul Parish, St. Peter Parish, St. Stephen Parish, and St. Thomas Parish.

Dublin (Roman Catholic or RC)

Rathmines Parish, SS. Michael & John Parish, St. Andrew Parish, St. Catherine Parish, St. Mary, Pro Cathedral Parish, and St. Nicholas Parish.

Hurst

ꜰamilies

- Andrew Burdett & Jane Unknown

  - Anne Burdett – bapt. 1830 (Baptism, **St. Andrew Parish (RC)**)

  - Andrew Burdett – bapt. 1832 (Baptism, **St. Andrew Parish (RC)**)

- Arthur Burdett & Anne Burdett

  - Mary Jane Burdett – b. 1812, bapt. 30 May 1812 (Baptism, **St. George Parish**)

  - Adelaide Louisa Burdett – bapt. 13 Aug 1817 (Baptism, **St. George Parish**)

- Arthur Burdett & Unknown

  - Arthur Burdett & Grace Florinda Trench – 25 Mar 1862 (Marriage, **St. Mary Parish**)

Signatures:

Arthur Burdett (son):

Residence - Hunstanton, King's County - March 25, 1862

Occupation - Gentleman - March 25, 1862

Grace Florinda Trench, daughter of John Eyre Trench (daughter-in-law):

Residence - 44 Rutland Square - March 25, 1862

Hurst

John Eyre Trench (father):

Occupation - Gentleman

Arthur Burdett (father):

Occupation - Barrister at Law

Wedding Witnesses:

John Eyre Trench & Charles O'Hara Trench

Signatures:

- Arthur Burdett & Unknown
  - Arthur Florian Hugo Burdett & Henrietta Maude St. George – 23 Jul 1884 (Marriage, **St. Anne Parish**)

Signatures:

- Grace Sophia Burdett – b. 21 Dec 1885, bapt. 21 Jan 1886 (Baptism, **St. Stephen Parish**)

Burdett Surname Ireland: 1600s to 1900s

Arthur Florian Hugo Burdett (son):

Residence - Coolpin, Banagher, King's County - July 23, 1884

98 Lower Baggot Street - January 21, 1886

Occupation - Esquire - July 23, 1884

Captain [Hard to Read] - January 21, 1886

Henrietta Maude St. George, daughter of Robert St. George (daughter-in-law):

Residence - Ivy Lodge, Ballingoloe, Co. Galway - July 23, 1884

Robert St. George (father):

Occupation - Esquire

Arthur Burdett (father):

Occupation - Esquire

Wedding Witnesses:

Ernest Wyndham Barnard & Robert James Kerr St. George

Signatures:

Hurst

- George Burdett & Jane Bridges – 13 Aug 1775 (Marriage, **St. Anne Parish**)

- George Burdett & Jane Burdett

  - Arthur Burdett – bapt. 11 Apr 1770 (Baptism, **St. Mary Parish**)

George Burdett (father):

Occupation - Esquire - April 11, 1770

- George Burdett & Sarah Burdett

  - George Burdett – bur. 21 Dec 1671 (Burial, **St. Michan Parish**)

- Henry Burdett & Sibella Burdett

Signature:

  - Louisa Jane Burdett – b. 18 Sep 1861, bapt. 11 Oct 1861 (Baptism, **St. Mary Parish**)

Henry Burdett (father):

Residence - Newbliss, Co. Monaghan - October 11, 1861

Occupation - Clergyman - October 11, 1861

- James Burdett & Catherine Cavanagh – 29 Nov 1837 (Marriage, **St. Andrew Parish** (RC))

  - Elizabeth Burdett – bapt. 1848 (Baptism, **St. Andrew Parish** (RC))

  - Catherine Burdett – bapt. 1853 (Baptism, **St. Andrew Parish** (RC))

Wedding Witnesses:

Michael Gormly & Thomas Grehaw

Burdett Surname Ireland: 1600s to 1900s

- John Burdett & Margaret Burdett

  - John Burdett – bur. 27 Feb 1694 (Burial, **St. Michan Parish**)

  - William Burdett – bapt. 9 Feb 1696 (Baptism, **St. Michan Parish**)

  - Elizabeth Burdett – bur. 4 Oct 1697 (Burial, **St. Michan Parish**)

  - Arthur Burdett – bapt. 15 Jul 1698 (Baptism, **St. Paul Parish**)

  - Richard Burdett – bur. 24 Apr 1700 (Burial, **St. Michan Parish**)

John Burdett (father):

Occupation - Dean - February 27, 1694

October 4, 1697

- John Burdett, b. 1776, bur. 11 Sep 1841 (Burial, **St. Mary Parish**) & Unknown

  - Arthur Michael Burdett – b. 1816, bur. 4 Feb 1847 (Burial, **St. Mary Parish**)

Arthur Michael Burdett (son):

Residence - 44 Rutland Square - before February 4, 1847

Age at Death - 31 years

  - Francis Robert Burdett – b. 1822, bur. 30 Nov 1843 (Burial, **St. Mary Parish**)

Francis Robert Burdett (son):

Residence - Rutland Square, West - before November 30, 1843

Age at Death - 21 years

○ Louisa Burdett & Michael Dawes – 17 Jun 1845 (Marriage, **St. George Parish**)

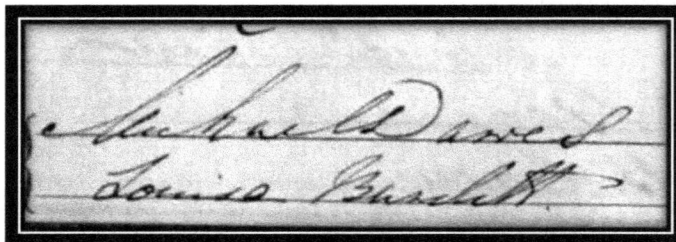

Signatures:

Louisa Burdett (daughter):

 Residence - 44 Rutland Square - June 17, 1845

 Occupation - Gentlewoman - June 17, 1845

Michael Dawes, son of Daniel Butler Dawes (son-in-law):

 Residence - 7 Eccles Street - June 17, 1845

 Occupation - Captain in the Indian Army - June 17, 1845

Daniel Butler Dawes (father):

 Occupation - Esquire

John Burdett (father):

 Occupation - Clergyman

Burdett Surname Ireland: 1600s to 1900s

Wedding Witnesses:

Henry Burdett & John Eyre Trench

Signatures:

John Burdett (father):

   Residence - 44 Rutland Square, West - before September 11, 1841

   Occupation - Reverend - before September 11, 1841

   Age at Death - 65 years

- Joseph Burdett & Unknown

   o Mary Burdett & Thomas Ryder – 29 Jul 1858 (Marriage, **St. Mary Parish**)

Signatures:

Hurst

Mary Burdett (daughter):

Residence - 20 Jervis Street - July 29, 1858

Thomas Ryder, son of William Ryder (father):

Residence - Kingstown - July 29, 1858

Occupation - Policeman - July 29, 1858

William Ryder (father):

Occupation - Mason

Joseph Burdett (father):

Occupation - Gardener

Wedding Witnesses:

Robert Cowan & Mary Cowan

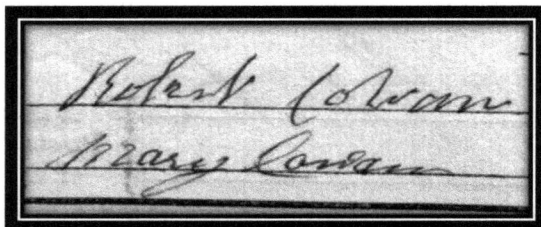

Signatures:

- Michael Burdett & Eleanor Unknown
  - Mary Burdett – bapt. 1795 (Baptism, **St. Andrew Parish** (RC))

- Michael Burdett & Elizabeth Redmond
  - Elizabeth Burdett – b. 1863, bapt. 1863 (Baptism, **St. Andrew Parish** (RC))
  - Anne Burdett – b. 1866, bapt. 1866 (Baptism, **St. Andrew Parish** (RC))

Burdett Surname Ireland: 1600s to 1900s

Michael Burdett (father):

Residence - 4 Prince's Street - 1863

13 Boyne Street - 1866

- Michael Burdett & Unknown

  o Mary Burdett & Daniel Booth – 2 May 1887 (Marriage, **St. Andrew Parish** (RC))

    ▪ Patrick Michael Booth – b. 1890, bapt. 1890 (Baptism, **St. Andrew Parish** (RC))

    ▪ Elizabeth Booth – b. 1892, bapt. 1892 (Baptism, **St. Andrew Parish** (RC))

    ▪ Michael John Booth – b. 1894, bapt. 1894 (Baptism, **St. Andrew Parish** (RC))

Mary Burdett (daughter):

Residence - 11 Cumberland - May 2, 1887

Daniel Booth, son of Daniel Booth (son-in-law):

Residence - 82 Townsend Street - May 2, 1887

Cumberland Street - 1890

9 South Cumberland Street - 1892

1894

Wedding Witnesses:

Thomas Foss & Anne Ward

  o John Burdett & Sarah Fox – 30 Jul 1888 (Marriage, **St. Andrew Parish** (RC))

John Burdett (son):

Residence - 9 Cumberland Street - July 30, 1888

Hurst

Sarah Fox, daughter of Matthew Fox (daughter-in-law):

Residence - 193 Brunswick Street - July 30 1888

Wedding Witnesses:

Margaret Murtagh & Daniel Booth

- Thomas Burdett & Bridgett Burdett

  o Thomas Burdett – b. 27 Jan 1744, bapt. 31 Jan 1744 (Baptism, Carlow Parish)

  o Elizabeth Burdett – bur. 19 Mar 1745 (Burial, Carlow Parish)

  o Anne Burdett – b. 9 Aug 1747, bapt. 13 Aug 1747 (Baptism, Carlow Parish)

  o Hugh Burdett – b. 20 Oct 1749, bapt. 22 Oct 1749 (Baptism, Carlow Parish), d. 19 Jun 1750, bur. 20 Jun 1750 (Burial, Carlow Parish)

- Thomas Burdett & Catherine Gockin

  o John Burdett – bapt. 13 Mar 1814 (Baptism, Lislee, Abbeymahon & Donoughmore (Barryroe) Parish (RC))

- Thomas Burdett & Mary Margaret McBride

  o Francis Burdett – bapt. Jan 1821 (Baptism, St. Nicholas Parish (RC))

  o Michael Burdett – bapt. 17 Apr 1826 (Baptism, SS. Michael & John Parish (RC))

  o John Burdett – bapt. Nov 1828 (Baptism, SS. Michael & John Parish (RC))

  o Elizabeth Burdett – bapt. 14 Mar 1832 (Baptism, St. Catherine Parish (RC))

- Thomas Burdett & Mary Burdett

  o Elizabeth Burdett & Patrick McNulty – 25 May 1861 (Marriage, St. Mary, Pro Cathedral Parish (RC))

    ▪ Mary McNulty – b. 1862, bapt. 1862 (Baptism, St. Andrew Parish (RC))

Burdett Surname Ireland: 1600s to 1900s

Elizabeth Burdett (daughter):

Residence - 15 Capel Street - May 25, 1861

Patrick McNulty, son of Terence McNulty & Margaret McNulty (son-in-law):

Residence - 7 Rutland Hill - May 25, 1861

George's Street - 1862

Wedding Witnesses:

Peter McHick & Ellen Bird

- Unknown Burdett & M. Burdett, bur. 30 Oct 1721 (Burial, **St. Patrick Parish**)

Unknown Burdett (husband):

Occupation - Major - October 30, 1721

- Unknown Burdett & Unknown
  - o Francis Burdett

Signature:

Francis Burdett (son):

Occupation - Major, 17th Lancers

- Unknown Burdett & Unknown

  o James Burdett

Signature:

- Unknown Burdett & Unknown

  o Jane Burdett

Signature:

- Unknown Burdett & Unknown

  o Thomas Burdett

Signature:

- William Burdett & Catherine Unknown

  o Anne Burdett – bapt. 17 Nov 1731 (Baptism, **St. Peter Parish**)

  o Thomas Burdett – b. 27 Oct 1734, bapt. 9 Nov 1734 (Baptism, **St. Peter Parish**)

- William Burdett & Dorcas Beard – 3 Sep 1759 (Marriage, **St. Anne Parish**)

Burdett Surname Ireland: 1600s to 1900s

- William Burdett & Unknown

  o Thomas Burdett – bur. 10 Mar 1755 (Burial, **Carlow Parish**)

William Burdett (father):

Title - Sir

- William Vigers Burdett & Henrietta O'Loughlin – 5 Oct 1769 (Marriage, **St. Andrew Parish**)

  o William Bagenal Burdett – bapt. 16 Jul 1770 (Baptism, **Carlow Parish**)

William Vigers Burdett (father):

Title - Sir

Individual Baptisms/Births

None Were Listed

Individual Burials

- Anne Burdett – b. 1743, bur. 20 Nov 1824 (Burial, St. Mary Parish)

Anne Burdett (deceased):

   Residence - Co. Cavan - before November 20, 1824

   Age at Death - 81 years

- Arthur Burdett – bur. 12 Sep 1768 (Burial, St. Mary Parish)

Arthur Burdett (deceased):

   Residence - Henry Street - before September 12, 1768

   Occupation - Esquire - before September 12, 1768

- Elizabeth Burdett [Miss] – bur. 19 Jun 1807 (Burial, St. Mary Parish)

Elizabeth Burdett (deceased):

   Residence - Palace Row - before June 19, 1807

- George Burdett – bur. 5 Feb 1818 (Burial, St. Mary Parish)

George Burdett (deceased):

   Residence - Great George's Street - before February 5, 1818

   Occupation - Esquire - before February 5, 1818

Hurst

- Jane Burdett – bur. 8 Sep 1722 (Burial, **St. Nicholas Without Parish**)

Jane Burdett (deceased):

   Residence - Francis Street - before September 8, 1722

- Jane Burdett – b. 1823, d. 19 Oct 1824, bur. 1824 (Burial, **St. Peter Parish**)

Jane Burdett (deceased):

   Residence - Whitefriar Street - October 19, 1824

   Age at Death - 1 year

- Mary Burdett – b. 1782, bur. 8 Jul 1816 (Burial, **Clontarf Parish**)

Mary Burdett (deceased):

   Residence - Clontarf Parish - before July 8, 1816

   Title - Lady

- Mary Burdett – b. 1755, bur. 28 Oct 1835 (Burial, **St. Peter Parish**)

Mary Burdett (deceased):

   Residence - 110 Stephen's Green - before October 28, 1835

   Age at Death - 80 years

   Place of Burial - St. Peter's Cemetery

Burdett Surname Ireland: 1600s to 1900s

- Unknown Burdett – bur. 9 Apr 1723 (Burial, **St. Nicholas Without Parish**)

Unknown Burdett (deceased):

   Residence - Patrick Street - before April 9, 1723

   Occupation - Shoemaker - before April 9, 1723

- Unknown Burdett – bur. 24 Feb 1733 (Burial, **St. Nicholas Without Parish**)

Unknown Burdett (deceased):

   Residence - Plunkett Street - before February 24, 1733

- Unknown Burdett (Child) – bur. 16 Oct 1767 (Burial, **St. Mary Parish**)

Unknown Burdett (Child) (deceased):

   Place of Burial - Parish Vault

- Unknown Burdett (Miss) – bur. 24 Jun 1755 (Burial, **St. Mary Parish**)

Unknown Burdett (Miss) (deceased):

   Residence - Henry Street - before June 24, 1755

- Unknown Burdett (Miss) – bur. 18 Apr 1767 (Burial, **St. Mary Parish**)

Unknown Burdett (Miss) (deceased):

   Residence - Henry Street - before April 18, 1767

Hurst

- Unknown Burdett (Mr.) – bur. Dec 1796 (Burial, **St. Mary Parish**)

Unknown Burdett (Mr.) (deceased):

   Residence - Cliane, Co. Kildare - before December 1796

   Occupation - Esquire - before December 1796

- Unknown Burdett (Mrs.) – bur. 8 May 1755 (Burial, **St. Mary Parish**)

Unknown Burdett (Mrs.) (deceased):

   Residence - Henry Street - before May 8, 1755

- Unknown Burdett (Mrs.) – bur. 5 May 1809 (Burial, **St. Mary Parish**)

Unknown Burdett (Mrs.) (deceased):

   Residence - George's Street - before May 5, 1809

Individual Marriages

- Anne Burdett & Thomas Kingsberry

  o Mary Josephine Kingsberry – b. 1899, bapt. 1899 (Baptism, **St. Andrew Parish** (RC))

Thomas Kingsberry (father):

Residence - Holles Street Hospital - 1899

- Grace Burdett & Henry P. L'Estrange

  o Grace Mary O'Mahony – b. 1818, bapt. 20 Dec 1856 (Baptism, **St. Mary, Pro Cathedral Parish**

  (RC))

Henry P. L'Estrange (father):

Residence - 38 Upper Rutland Street - December 20, 1856

- Mary Anne Burdett & Terence Meehan – 8 Aug 1852 (Marriage, **St. Nicholas Parish** (RC))

Wedding Witnesses:

Francis Meehan & Elizabeth Burdett

Hurst

- Sarah Burdett & Frederick Eagan

    o   Catherine Eagan – b. 1875, bapt. 1875 (Baptism, **St. Andrew Parish (RC)**)

Frederick Eagan (father):

Residence - 11 Stephen's Lane - 1875

- Teresa Burdett & Joseph Connor

    o   Josephine Connor – bapt. 3 May 1849 (Baptism, **Rathmines Parish (RC)**)

Burdett Surname Ireland: 1600s to 1900s

Name Variations

Includes Latin and Abbreviated forms of names found in the original documents.

Abigail = Abigale, Abigall

Anne = Ann, Anna, Annae

Bartholomew = Barth, Bartholmeus, Bartholomeo

Bridget = Birgis, Brigid, Brigida, Bridgit

Catherine = Catharine, Catharina, Catharinae, Catherina, Cath, Catha, Cathae, Cathe, Cathn, Kate

Charles = Carolus, Charls, Chas

Christopher = Christoph

Daniel = Danielem, Danielis

Edmund = Edmond

Edward = Ed, Edwd

Eleanor = Eleo, Eleonora, Elinor, Ellenor

Elizabeth = Betty, Elisa, Elisabeth, Eliz, Eliza, Elizab, Elizh, Elizth

Ellen = Elena, Ellena

Emily = Emilia

Esther = Essie, Ester

Francis = Fransicum

George = Geo, Georg, Georgius

Grace = Gratiae

Gulielmo = Guil, Guillelmi, Gulielmum, Guillelmus, Gulmi

Helen = Helena

Burdett Surname Ireland: 1600s to 1900s

Honor = Hanora, Honora

James = Jacobi, Jacobus, Jas

Jane = Joanna

Jeanne = Jeannae, Joannae

Joan = Johanna, Joney

John = Jno, Joannem, Joannes, Johannis

Joseph = Jos

Juliana = Julian

Leticia = Letitia, Lettice, Letticia

Lewis = Louis

Luke = Lucas

Margaret = Margarita, Margaritae, Margeret, Marget, Margt

Martha = Marthae

Mary = Maria, My

Mary Anne = Marianna, Marianne, Maryanne

Michael = Michaelis, Michl

Patrick = Pat, Patt, Patk, Patricii, Patricius

Peter = Petri

Richard = Ricardi, Ricardus, Rich, Richd

Robert = Roberti

Rose = Rosa, Rosae

Thomas = Thom, Thomae, Thoms, Thos, Ths

Timothy = Timotheus, Timy

William = Wil, Will, Willm, Wm

Notes

Notes

Notes

Notes

Notes

Notes

Index

B

Burdett Surname Ireland: 1600s to 1900s

Hurst

C

D

Burdett Surname Ireland: 1600s to 1900s

E

Eagan
  Baptisms
    Catherine
      1875 20
  Births
    Catherine
      1875 20
    Frederick... 20

F

Fox
  Matthew.. 10
  Sarah.. 9

G

Gockin
  Catherine 10

K

Kingsberry
  Baptisms
    Mary Josephine
      1899 19
  Births
    Mary Josephine
      1899 19
    Thomas 19

L

L'Estrange
  Henry P... 19

M

McBride
  Mary Margaret....................................... 10
McNulty
  Baptisms
    Mary
      1862 10
  Births
    Mary
      1862 10
    Patrick... 10
  Spouses
    Margaret.. 11
    Terence 11
Meehan
  Terence 19

O

O'Loughlin
  Henrietta 13
O'Mahony
  Baptisms
    Grace Mary
      1856 Dec 20 19
  Births
    Grace Mary
      1818 19

R

S

T

U

About The Author

Donovan Hurst graduated from San Diego State University with a Bachelor of Arts in the major field of studies of History and a minor in the field of studies of Anthropology. He is a current member of The General Society of Mayflower Descendants and has been conducting genealogical research for over 10 years tracing back his ancestors to their ancestral homelands in Denmark, England, France, Germany, Ireland, Norway, and Scotland.

www.ingramcontent.com/pod-product-compliance
Lightning Source LLC
Chambersburg PA
CBHW081204270326
41930CB00014B/3295